DATE DUE			

DIGGING UP
TYRANNOSAURUS REX

John R. Horner & Don Lessem

CROWN PUBLISHERS, INC., New York

To the Wankel family

Published by Crown Publishers, Inc., a Random
House company, 201 East 50th Street, New York,
New York 10022

CROWN is a trademark of Crown Publishers, Inc.

Manufactured in Hong Kong

Library of Congress Cataloging-in-Publication Data
Horner, John R.
Digging up Tyrannosaurus rex / John R. Horner &
Don Lessem.
p. cm.
Includes bibliographical references and index.
Summary: Describes the discovery and excavation of
the world's only complete Tyrannosaurus fossil in
Montana, and what was learned from it.
1. Tyrannosaurus rex—Juvenile literature.
[1. Tyrannosaurus rex. 2. Dinosaurs. 3. Fossils.
4. Paleontology.] I. Lessem, Don. II. Title.
QE862.S3H67   1992
567.9'7—dc20   92-2204

ISBN 0-517-58783-1 (trade)
      0-517-58784-X (lib. bdg.)
      0-517-88336-8 (pbk.)
10 9 8 7 6 5 4 3 2 1

First paperback edition: March 1995

▲ *Tyrannosaurus rex* confronts
Triceratops in this 1930 painting by artist Charles R.
Knight in the Field Museum
of Natural History in Chicago.

*I*magine you are in a dinosaur world. It is 65 million years ago, at the end of the dinosaur era. Vast herds of duck-billed dinosaurs like *Edmontosaurus* and horned dinosaurs like *Triceratops* roam a warm and lush American West. These plant-eaters are as large as trucks. Yet one of them might have made just a single meal for the roaring, earthshaking giant that is approaching. It is the most terrifying animal that ever lived: *Tyrannosaurus rex*.

Tyrannosaurus rex stood 15 feet high and 40 feet long. Sharp teeth the size of bananas flashed from its jaws. With powerful neck and jaw muscles, it might have ripped off hunks of flesh as large as a human. The legs and tail of a tyrannosaur also could have delivered killing blows.

My name is Jack Horner. I read and imagined all these things about *Tyrannosaurus rex* when I was a boy growing up in Montana. But I wasn't just reading and imagining. Every summer, I searched the rocky badlands near my home for the bones of dinosaurs. I found a lot of them.

I still hunt for fossils—but now as a *paleontologist*, a scientist who studies the bones of ancient animals. My specialty is dinosaurs. For more than a century now, paleontologists like me have been digging up dinosaur bones.

Tyrannosaurus rex is one of the dinosaurs we've known about the longest. The first partial tyrannosaur skeletons were found in the early years of the twentieth century. Its size and terrifying appearance led to its being named "the tyrant lizard king."

▲ Movies have helped make *Tyrannosaurus rex* famous. But because only a very few fossils have been found, many images of *Tyrannosaurus rex* have been based on imagination.

These are the only *Tyrannosaurus rex* skeletons discovered so far that are more than 30% complete:

1. Wyoming, 1900. The first skeleton. It was originally called *Dynamosaurus imperiosus*. Now on display in the Natural History Museum in London, England. **2.** Eastern Montana, 1902. This half-complete skeleton was the one given the name *Tyrannosaurus rex*, by Dr. Henry Fairfield Osborn in 1905. Now in the Carnegie Museum, Pittsburgh. **3.** Eastern Montana, 1908. Missing legs and arms. In the American Museum of Natural History, New York City. **4.** Eastern Montana, 1966. Slightly more than half a skeleton. The skull is on display in the Los Angeles Museum of Natural History. **5.** Northwestern South Dakota, 1980. Less than half a skeleton. The skull is in the museum of the South Dakota School of Mines. **6.** Central Alberta, Canada, 1981. Less than half a skeleton. **7.** Southern Alberta, Canada, 1982. This skeleton was discovered by high-school students and is currently being studied at the Royal Tyrrell Museum of Palaeontology in Canada. **8.** Eastern Montana, 1988. Kathy Wankel's *Tyrannosaurus rex*, almost 90% complete. On display at the Museum of the Rockies, Bozeman, Montana. **9.** Western South Dakota, 1990. More than 90% complete and the largest known *Tyrannosaurus rex*. When cleaned, it will be displayed at the Black Hills Institute, Hill City, South Dakota. **10.** South Dakota, 1992. Black Hills Institute began excavating a fossil that is at least 60% complete.

But the truth is, we hardly know *Tyrannosaurus rex* at all. In the nearly 100 years following the first discovery, paleontologists found only a handful more skeletons of *Tyrannosaurus rex*. And none of them was much more than half-complete.

Without a nearly complete skeleton, we can't begin to understand how an animal looked, moved, and behaved. Because scientists had only bits and pieces of *Tyrannosaurus rex* to examine, many of the "facts" about *Tyrannosaurus rex* I learned as a child were actually only guesses. It might have been 40 feet long, or 50 feet long, or more. No one had found enough of its tail or body to know for sure. Did *Tyrannosaurus rex* have tiny arms too short to reach its mouth, the way it is always portrayed? That, too, was a guess, for no one had ever found all of the arm bones of a *Tyrannosaurus rex*.

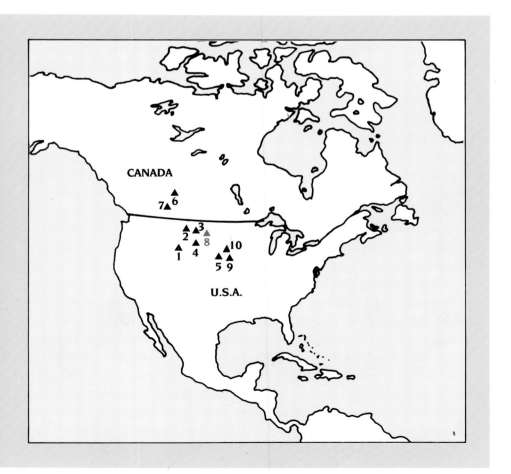

▲ The discovery of one of the first *Tyrannosaurus rex* fossils in eastern Montana in 1908. The bottom picture shows the quarry where the fossil was found. Above, the pelvic bones are being boxed for transport. The fossil was later put on display at the American Museum of Natural History in New York City (*see page* 31).

5

As a scientist, I want to know all I can about an animal. But to begin to know what *Tyrannosaurus rex* truly looked like, how it evolved, and how it lived, I need more information. In other words—more fossils. But I wasn't sure I, or anyone else, would find them.

Then, in 1988, a rancher named Kathy Wankel brought me some fossils. Kathy had gone for a walk with her family in the badlands of eastern Montana one morning that fall. The Wankels live way out in the wilds, nearly a hundred miles from the nearest town. Kathy likes to look for fossils on her hikes. On that day she walked onto a small hilltop and saw the tips of some brownish bones sticking out of the ground.

Kathy thought the bones belonged to a dinosaur, but she wasn't sure which part of what kind of dinosaur she had found. So Kathy brought the bones to the Museum of the Rockies, in Bozeman, Montana, which is where I work.

▼ The badlands of eastern Montana. The rocks exposed on the earth's surface here were made 65 million years ago, when *Tyrannosaurus rex* lived and died.

▼ Kathy Wankel and family.

◄ The arm bones of *Tyrannosaurus rex*, in a photograph taken after the excavation had been completed. Kathy Wankel, her husband Tom, and paleontologist Pat Leiggi look on.

As soon as I saw the bones, I knew Kathy had found something very unusual. From their size and shape, I could tell right away that these were the upper and lower arm bones of a *big* animal. And I had a pretty good idea whose arm bones they were. They were thicker than any dinosaur arm bones I'd ever seen. And these bones had originally been hollow (although as fossils they had become filled in with rock). Only meat-eating dinosaurs had hollow bones.

Other scientists had established many years ago that the rocks in the badlands where Kathy had been walking were laid down about 65 million years ago. It is one of the few places in North America where rocks of that age are exposed. At that time, there was only one meat-eating animal big enough to have arm bones like those I was holding: *Tyrannosaurus rex*!

I'm not the kind of person who hops up and down when I find something special. But I was pretty excited to think I was holding the first arm bones of *Tyrannosaurus rex* that had *ever* been found.

I knew, too, that Kathy had just scratched the surface of her find. There was a chance that underneath and around these arm bones lay much more of the animal. I was eager to find out if there were other missing clues to the true nature of *Tyrannosaurus rex* buried in the Montana badlands.

I sent my chief assistant, Pat Leiggi, and three expert helpers to explore the site. The land the bones were on is a wildlife refuge that belongs to the United States government. Before he could prospect for dinosaur bones, Pat had to get the permission of government officials. The government was a great help. Later, army engineers even built a dirt road to help us get our trucks and equipment to the site.

Pat and his crew weren't sure how many bones lay near the surface, so they began looking for *Tyrannosaurus rex* using very small tools—awls and little trowels. They wanted to be careful not to chip away any of the delicate bone by accident. But no other bones lay near the surface, so the crew began digging through the sandstone with picks and shovels. Soon they came upon some very large bones. Now Pat knew there were many bones in the hill, but he couldn't yet be sure if they came from one or from many dinosaurs.

▼ Part of the *Tyrannosaurus rex* skull, exposed by Pat Leiggi's crew during the first dig.

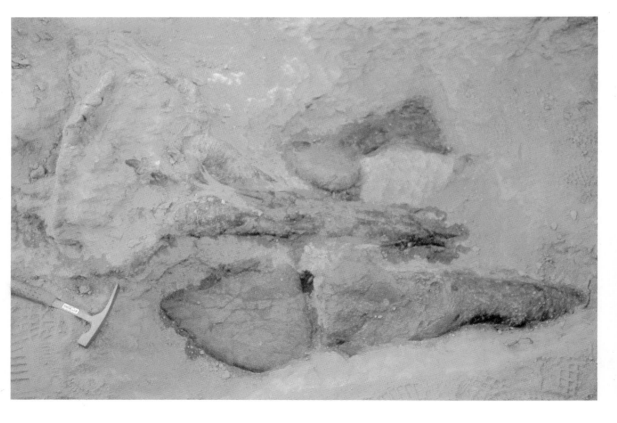

As paleontologists always do, Pat mapped the position of the bones he'd found. That information might one day tell us how the bones became preserved. Perhaps several dinosaurs died beside a river, and the current heaped their bones together. Or maybe one dinosaur died in the water and was quickly covered over with mud.

Pat could make out the backbone, hips, and skull of a dinosaur so big and toothy it could only be *Tyrannosaurus rex*. He was eager to find out how much of the animal lay in the hillside.

But time was running out. Winter was coming. The bones the crew had partly exposed needed to be protected from wind and freezing rain. They also had to be hidden from people who collect fossils without permission. Pat and his crew wrapped the bones in strips of burlap soaked in plaster. The plaster dried over the fabric to make a huge, hard cast. Pat covered the plaster with dirt to hide the skeleton.

The following June, Pat and I came back with ten of our expert fossil diggers from the Museum of the Rockies. We weren't sure how much of *Tyrannosaurus rex* or other dinosaurs we would find, but we did know that any fossils we found would lie beneath many feet of hard rock. The rock on top of the bones is called *overburden*. We used jackhammers to break it into big blocks. Then we used crowbars and our bare hands to roll these huge blocks down the hill. In all, we moved more than 150 tons of rocks this way in just a few days. Our backs were very sore.

At last we got down close to the layer of rock that hid the bones. The material surrounding a fossil is called *matrix*. In this case, the matrix was sandstone. It was soft and crumbly—and so were the bones within it. So we began to scrape away the rock with awls, always being careful not to hit a bone with our tools. Soon dull brown bone began to show all over the hilltop. As the bones appeared, we poured clear glue over them. The glue soaked into the bones and made them harder and shinier.

▲ Glue is poured over the exposed bones to protect them.

► With a dozen fossil diggers working all day, the outline of the *Tyrannosaurus rex* fossil was soon visible on the hillside.

Soon we could make out a long row of back bones (called *vertebrae*), a leg bone, and the huge bones of a dinosaur's hips. Near one hip we found much of *Tyrannosaurus rex*'s 4½-foot-long skull, with its huge teeth still poking menacingly from its jaw. As work progressed, we identified individual bones that added up to the nearly complete and curled body of a single specimen of *Tyrannosaurus rex*. Stretched out, that animal would have been 40 feet long. Parts of the skull, legs, tail, and one arm were either hidden or missing. But in two weeks of digging, we'd revealed more of *Tyrannosaurus rex* than anyone had ever seen before.

As the bones were identified, their positions were precisely marked on a quarry map. As we exposed more and more, a picture emerged of how this animal died and was buried.

We know that the animal must have been buried because, to be preserved as fossils, bones must be covered over by mud or sand soon after the animal dies. Then the bones must be protected from decay for many thousands of years while minerals seep into the bones and turn them into fossils.

Left: The giant upper leg bone of *Tyrannosaurus rex*. The bones to the right of the leg bone belong to the skull. *Right*: The backbone runs from the top to the bottom of this picture, with the neck at the top and the tail at the bottom.

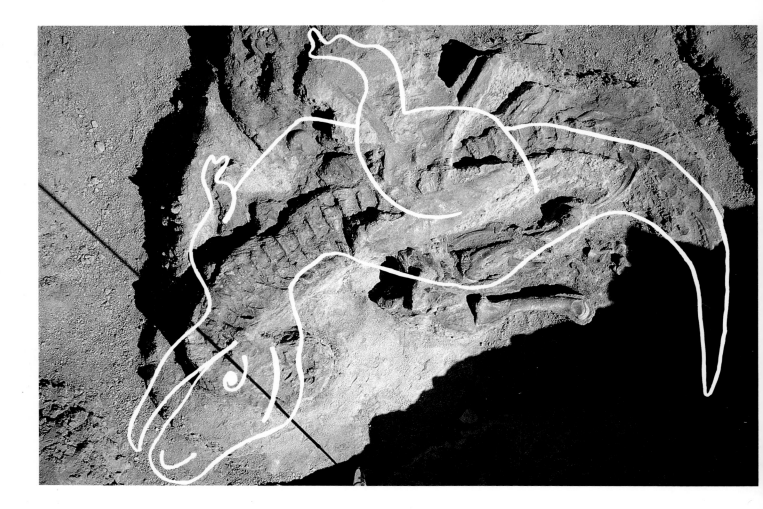

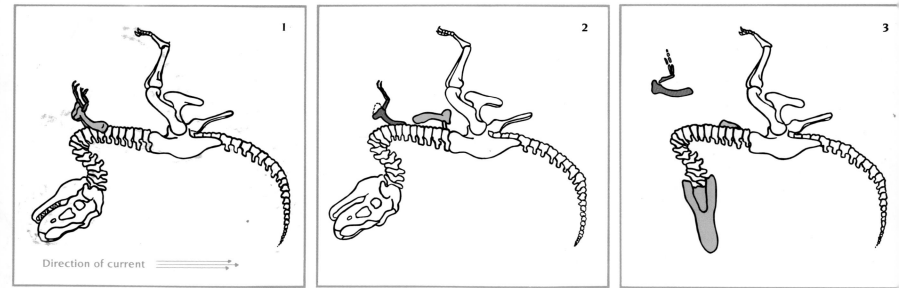

Direction of current

A view of the complete fossil from above. The outline shows the position of *Tyrannosaurus rex* when it died.

▼ After the muscle and skin had rotted away (**1**), the current in the stream washed the right arm under the backbone. The bones of the left arm were washed several feet away, where they were found by Kathy Wankel (**2–3**). The head separated from the neck: the skull rolled against the hip bones and the lower jaw ended up by the tail (**4**). The bones of the right leg flipped over and separated (**5–6**). The small bones of the feet and the tail were washed away.

We don't know what killed this animal. Unlike some other dinosaur bones, these didn't show any big bite marks, scars, or lumps that would have indicated this animal had been injured in any way.

We do know that this dinosaur was washed gently into a stream not long after it died. We can tell that because it was buried in sandstone, rock that is made from sand. The current in the stream must have been gentle, because most of the bones were *articulated*—that means they were still lined up as they would have been in the living animal's skeleton.

But some things had changed since the animal died; its head was curled toward its back. That happens to all animals after they die, as their neck muscles tighten.

This animal ended up lying on its left side. The current in the stream washed some bones out of position. Bones of the left arm ended up several feet away. The skull separated from the lower jaw and rolled up against the pelvic bones. The bones of the right leg flipped over and separated. The small, light bones at the end of the tail and those of the feet must have washed away.

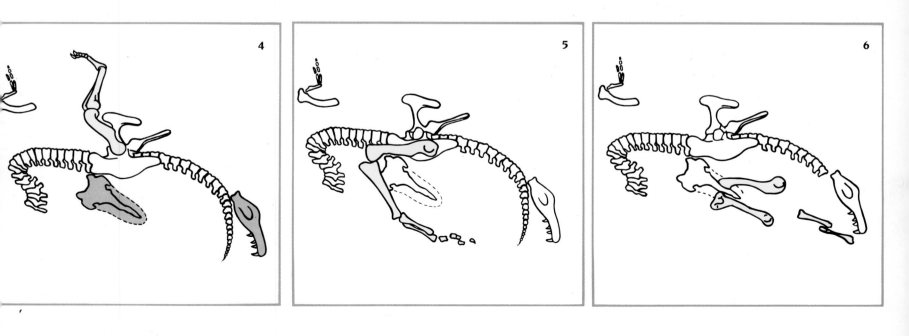

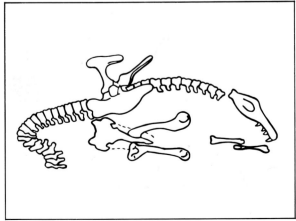

▲ The exposed *Tyrannosaurus rex* skeleton. The hip bones are in the center, the neck on the left, and the tail on the right. The leg bones and parts of the skull are below and to the right of the hip bones.

► A trench is made around the fossil so that diggers can tunnel underneath it.

Once we had dug several feet out from the farthest bones without finding any more, we were pretty sure we'd found all the bones we could expect to collect. We began to tunnel underneath the bones, so that they stood on a *pedestal*, like a statue in an art museum.

As we tunneled, we tried to separate the bones into groups without cutting into any of them. Each bundle of bones had to be small enough to fit into the museum. With an animal the size of *Tyrannosaurus rex*, that wasn't easy.

The delicate skull bones looked as though they had washed right into the dinosaur's huge hips. We were afraid we might not be able to separate the skull into its own bundle without damaging its bones. Skulls are particularly important to us. They're rare and full of information about an animal's senses, its looks, and its evolution from earlier animals. With my awl and shovel, I tunneled under the skull and found a fraction of an inch of dirt I could scrape away between the skull and hips. It was big relief to know we could move the skull without harming it.

▼ Removing the rock between the skull and the hips.

But before we could move the skull and all the other bones, we first had to wrap them. We soaked more burlap bandages in plaster and wrapped the tops and sides of the fossils many times over. In a few days, we had separated all the bones into ten bundles, without breaking a single one.

The army loaned us backhoes and trucks to move the huge packages of bones. None of us had ever tried to lift anything so big and lumpy—and delicate—so we moved *Tyrannosaurus rex* very slowly and carefully.

First we tied heavy straps around the packages of bones. We hoisted them with chains, and wrapped and plastered them thoroughly underneath. Then we placed the bundles onto wooden platforms and slid them onto the back of a big flatbed truck. The bone bundles were hauled out to a smooth road and from there were lifted onto an even bigger truck.

The moving process was a lot harder than any of us had imagined it would be. Although we had made the bundles as small as we could, some of them weighed several tons. Some platforms snapped under the great weight, and once one of the backhoe's huge back wheels was lifted right off the ground.

◀ The sound of wood cracking brings workers running to check this platform as it is hoisted onto the truck.

It had taken us a month to prepare the bundles and a whole day to lift them onto the truck. Now, for the first time in 65 million years, *Tyrannosaurus rex* was on the move again. But our work had only begun.

We drove *Tyrannosaurus rex* 350 miles back to the museum in the middle of a fierce thunderstorm, but it arrived without a scratch. We had wanted to bring it right into our laboratory in the museum basement to begin picking away the tons of dirt still surrounding the bones. But some of the bone packages were so heavy that they would have cracked the floor of the museum. So we had to start breaking apart the bundles outside on the loading dock.

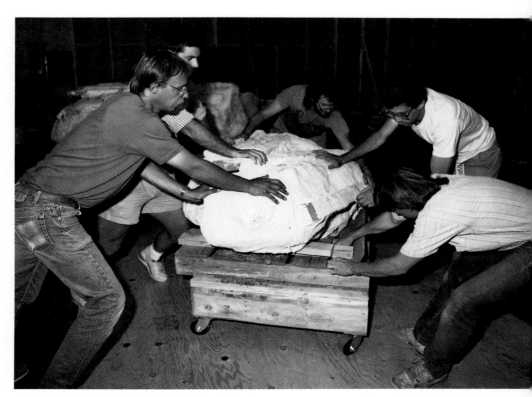

It took a few days to make the biggest fossil packages small enough to bring into the museum. We set up a special *Tyrannosaurus rex* laboratory behind a big glass window in the exhibition space of the museum. That way visitors to the museum could watch us working on the bones.

Cleaning and repairing a fossil is an incredibly slow and difficult process. As I write, several talented cleaners have been working on the fossil for nearly three years, and they aren't done yet. They began by sawing off the plaster jackets with a little saw like the one a doctor uses to cut a cast off a broken arm. It vibrates rapidly, but doesn't have a sharp blade that might cut your skin or a dinosaur bone.

Once the plastered burlap was removed, the cleaners chipped away at the dirt with little picks, much like those a dentist uses to clean teeth. In fact, a lot of our fossil-cleaning tools were made for dentists, not dinosaurs.

▲ Pat Leiggi chips away at the plaster surrounding a hip bone of *Tyrannosaurus rex*. In the foreground are some of the tools and brushes used in this delicate work.

Sometimes we clean fossils with a tiny jackhammer called an *air scribe*. It has a point as small as an ink pen, and it moves rapidly in and out, pecking away at the dirt. But the *Tyrannosaurus rex* and the sandstone around it were so soft we couldn't use an air scribe. Often just a little scrubbing with a small brush, such as a paintbrush, was enough to remove the dirt from around the bone.

Each bone was prepared separately. Often cracks were found where the bone had been broken. Sometimes rock was packed into the cracks. The cleaners removed all the rock, and if the fossil pieces that were left fit neatly back together, they were glued into place. But if even the smallest fragment of bone had disappeared, the remaining pieces were not reattached. We kept all the parts, but if we weren't sure how they fit together, we didn't put them together just on a hunch.

The first bones cleaned were those of the arm. We couldn't wait to see what the arms of *Tyrannosaurus rex* really looked like. Ken Carpenter and Matt Smith, two of our top workers, made a special study of the arms. They found that they were even stubbier than people had imagined. On a dinosaur 40 feet long, the arms were no longer than a human's. To our surprise, Matt and Ken discovered that, although the arms were small, they were a lot stronger than anyone had guessed.

The stubby arms of tyrannosaurs had always been pictured as uselessly weak. Matt and Ken measured the scars left on the bones in the places where the arm muscles once attached. From the size of one of those scars—a bump the size of a quarter—they could estimate how big the upper-arm muscles were. Then, by comparing the size of that muscle to the arm muscles of other animals, the researchers came up with an estimate of the strength of *Tyrannosaurus rex*. They calculated it could pull more than 440 pounds. That meant the *Tyrannosaurus rex*'s arms were almost ten times stronger than those of the average human.

► The smaller bones in the bottom half of this picture made up the arms of *Tyrannosaurus rex*. The large bone at the top is the shoulder bone. Although *Tyrannosaurus rex* was over 40 feet long, its arms were no bigger than a human's.

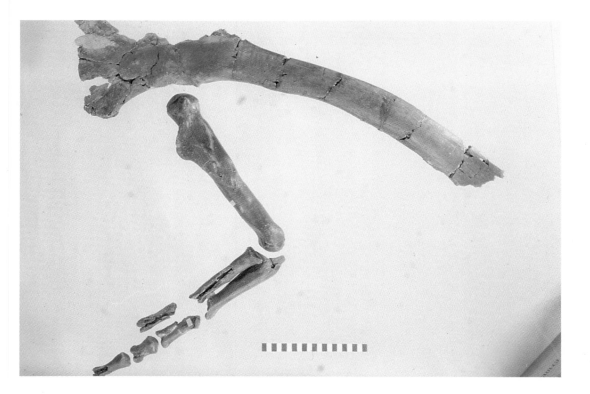

When Ken and Matt positioned the fingers, they made another surprising discovery. They found that *Tyrannosaurus rex*'s two claws were not lined up in parallel like the tines of a fork. Instead, the claws would have spread outward as they moved, like meat hooks, to grip prey.

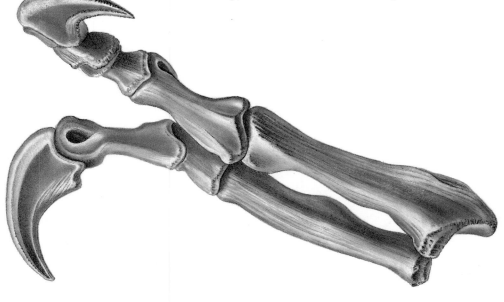

◄ A drawing of the forearm of *Tyrannosaurus rex*, based on the bones found by Kathy Wankel. Since no *Tyrannosaurus rex* claws have ever been found, these claws are based on those of *Albertosaurus*, a smaller meat-eating dinosaur that lived near to the time of *Tyrannosaurus rex*. As the *Tyrannosaurus rex* gripped its prey, the claws moved apart slightly.

► This painting, by artist Doug Henderson, is based on information from Kathy Wankel's discovery. It shows *Tyrannosaurus rex* striding through a forest of *Metasequoia* trees at sunset. Instead of being shown upright, as it was in earlier paintings like the one in the Field Museum (*see page* 2), *Tyrannosaurus rex* is in a horizontal posture with its tail out straight. Its arms are small and mostly hidden by the shoulder muscles.

So far, these studies of the *Tyrannosaurus rex* arm are the most dramatic results from our dig. We now know a part of its anatomy no one has ever seen before, and we have an idea of how it looked and functioned. But what *Tyrannosaurus rex* did with its powerful little arms remains a mystery. Matt and Ken think it might have used them to pin down a thrashing victim. I'm still not sure they were strong enough or long enough to hold down a living dinosaur. We do know that most of the upper arms of *Tyrannosaurus rex* would have been hidden by powerful shoulder muscles, so they would have looked even shorter on the living animal than we've pictured them in the past.

We're discovering a lot of other useful information from the *Tyrannosaurus rex* bones. We've finished cleaning all the skull bones, and we've measured them carefully and compared them with other *Tyrannosaurus rex* skulls. We'll do the same with the rest of the bones as they are prepared. As more *Tyrannosaurus rex* fossils are found, we may have enough different skeletons to be able to say something about how fast it grew, and whether a male tyrannosaur looked different from a female.

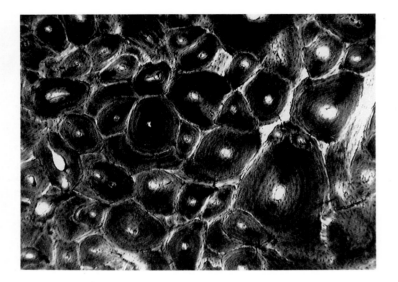

◄ A thin slice of *Tyrannosaurus rex* bone photographed under a microscope at 50X magnification. The dark areas are canals that contained blood vessels.

Meanwhile, we are taking small slices of bone and placing them under a microscope. As an animal grows up, the way in which it makes bone changes. The bone cells in adult animals are larger and thicker than those in young ones. From what we've seen so far of its bone structure, we can tell that this *Tyrannosaurus rex* was a grownup.

Perhaps one day we will have enough different-sized specimens of *Tyrannosaurus rex* to be able to figure out how old each one was from microscope studies of their bones.

The first *Tyrannosaurus rex* skeletons to be put on display in museums were made from actual fossil bones. Because we want to keep studying our *Tyrannosaurus rex* bones for many years, we are not going to put them together to make a display skeleton. Also, putting screws and bolts on the bones for a permanent exhibit would damage the fossils. We do, however, want to share our *Tyrannosaurus rex*, so we'll put the individual bones out for display.

When all the bones have been cleaned, we'll make replicas. Rubbery latex will be poured around each bone; when dry, the latex covering will be stripped off, making a mold. We'll fill the mold with liquid fiberglass or some other plastic. When it sets, we'll pop out an exact copy of a *Tyrannosaurus rex* bone. All those parts will be fitted together to make a *Tyrannosaurus rex* skeleton.

The first *Tyrannosaurus rex* skeletons put on display were also posed incorrectly. The one in the American Museum of Natural History, in New York City, stood for nearly a century upright, resting on a huge tail. But that's not how *Tyrannosaurus rex* actually stood. We know by the way in which our specimen's bones fit together that the animal leaned forward, with its tail off the ground. The bones won't go together any other way. But back in the early 1900s, the museum couldn't make its skeleton, with its heavy bones and iron supports, stand unless it was propped straight up. They added several extra feet of fake tail for balance. Now that lighter weight supports are available, the American Museum's scientists are changing the pose to a forward-leaning, tail-raised position.

▼

The *Tyrannosaurus rex* display that stood until 1992 in the American Museum of Natural History.

Other natural history museums have begun basing their *Tyrannosaurus rex* displays on modern fossil discoveries. The Royal Tyrrell Museum, in Alberta, Canada, is the world's largest fossil museum. Among its exhibits is a *Tyrannosaurus rex* skeleton with its head down and tail up, as if striding. The Academy of Natural Science, in Philadelphia, has created a similar active pose for its *Tyrannosaurus rex*.

The Denver Museum of Natural History has taken its *Tyrannosaurus rex* a step further. A skeleton cast from the bones in the American Museum, in New York City, has been posed in the midst of a high leg kick with its head turned sideways. The huge, open jaws of *Tyrannosaurus rex* greet visitors as they enter the fossil hall. This is a highly athletic vision of how *Tyrannosaurus rex* might have moved.

▼ The Royal Tyrrell Museum in Alberta, Canada.

▼ The Academy of Natural Sciences, Philadelphia.

▲ The Denver Museum of Natural History.

Right: This model, designed for a museum exhibit, was created by studying fossil skeletons and shows how *Tyrannosaurus rex* might have looked with muscle and skin covering its bones.

We haven't decided how we'll pose our *Tyrannosaurus rex* yet. I'd like to make two skeletons and pose them as if they were tearing up a dinosaur carcass. That's how the man who named *Tyrannosaurus rex*, the president of the American Museum of Natural History, Henry Fairfield Osborn, wanted to pose the first *Tyrannosaurus rex* display in the early 1900s. Today, we have the lightweight materials to build what couldn't be created for Osborn.

A new *Tyrannosaurus rex* exhibit will be a wonderful way to show visitors to the museum what we've learned from our fossil, from the animal's stubby arms to its long, elevated tail. But there is still a lot we don't know. Before we can say whether *Tyrannosaurus rex* was warm-blooded, fast-running, or a ferocious killer, we will need more information. That means more fossils.

◄
Pete Larson with the skull of the *Tyrannosaurus rex* his crew found in South Dakota in 1990.

Only a handful of *Tyrannosaurus rex* bones were found in the last century. No one has ever found a tyrannosaur baby or egg, discoveries that could tell us how tyrannosaurs developed. No one has found footprints that could tell us how fast tyrannosaurs moved.

But the same summer we dug up Kathy Wankel's *Tyrannosaurus rex*, another, even bigger *Tyrannosaurus rex* was discovered and excavated in South Dakota. In 1992 another *Tyrannosaurus rex*, nearly the size of Kathy Wankel's, was found in South Dakota. I think several more specimens will be found pretty soon. There are more trained and interested people out looking for fossils than ever before. And they know better where to look and what a *Tyrannosaurus rex* bone looks like.

Maybe you will come to the west and find a *Tyrannosaurus rex*. If you do, please call me right away. Together, we can dig it up.

▲ The crew that dug up *Tyran-nosaurus rex*, with the Wankel family.

RESOURCE GUIDE

The Big Beast Book, by Jerry Booth (Little, Brown). A unique combination of dinosaur facts and learning activities for older children.

Digging Dinosaurs, by John R. Horner and James Gorman (Workman). A grown-up book about one scientist's research into how dinosaurs lived.

Dinosaurs: A Golden Guide, by Dr. Eugene Gaffney (Golden Books). A handy and thorough pocket dinosaur reference.

The Illustrated Dinosaur Encyclopedia, by Dr. David Norman (Crescent Books). The best review of dinosaur evolution for any age; challenging reading for children, but beautifully illustrated by John Sibbick.

Maia: A Dinosaur Grows Up, by John R. Horner and James Gorman (Running Press). How a duck-billed dinosaur might have lived. With art by Doug Henderson.

The New Dinosaur Dictionary, by Helen Roney Sattler (Lothrop, Lee & Shepard). A good dinosaur-by-dinosaur summary.

The News About Dinosaurs, by Patricia Lauber (Bradbury Press). A brief review of recent theories about the way dinosaurs lived.

Tyrannosaurus Rex and Its Kin, by Helen Roney Sattler (Lothrop, Lee & Shepard). A brief overview of large carnivorous dinosaurs.

"T. rex Exposed." A PBS NOVA one-hour film that documents this *Tyrannosaurus rex* dig and describes what's known and what's speculated about *Tyrannosaurus rex* (Coronet Films).

Dino Times. A monthly newspaper for young people, published by: The Dinosaur Society, P.O. Box 87069, South Dartmouth, MA 02748.

INDEX

ABOUT THE AUTHORS

John R. ("Jack") Horner is curator of paleontology at the Museum of the Rockies at Montana State University, in Bozeman, Montana. Dr. Horner has made hundreds of dinosaur discoveries in Montana. He found the first dinosaur eggs discovered in North America and the first dinosaur embryos ever unearthed. He also uncovered the largest bed of dinosaur bones ever found, containing the fossils of thousands of duck-billed dinosaurs. Dr. Horner specializes in studying how duck-billed dinosaurs grew up and the environment in which they lived and evolved. With James Gorman, he is the coauthor of a children's book, *Maia: A Dinosaur Grows Up*, and an adult book, *Digging Dinosaurs*. He lives in Bozeman, Montana.

Don Lessem hosted a documentary about the discovery described in this book for the PBS television series NOVA. He has been on dinosaur digs in Mongolia, the Arctic, and numerous other places around the world; he has reported on paleontology and other science topics for the *Boston Globe*, the *New York Times*, *Life*, and other publications. His books include *Kings of Creation*, a survey of dinosaur discoveries around the world. Mr. Lessem is the founder and president of the Dinosaur Society, a nonprofit organization created to benefit dinosaur science, and the editor of *Dino Times*, a monthly newspaper for children published by the society. He lives in Waban, Massachusetts.